For three rogues:
an invitation to love art

THANKS TO THE MUSÉE DU LOUVRE AND ESPECIALLY TO :
Violaine Bouvet-Lanselle, publications director of the museum's cultural service,
for her encouragement, invaluable verification and attentive reading.
Marie-Claire Le Bourdellès and the Media Library team
Catherine Bridonneau, Department of Egyptian Antiquities
Marguerite Charritat, Department of Oriental Antiquities
Brigitte Ducrot, Objets d'art Department
Marie-Thérèse Génin, Painting Department
Agnès Scherer, Department of Greek and Roman Antiquities

MANY THANKS ALSO TO:
Diane Desazars for her efficient collaboration throughout this book's preparation
The Seuil jeunesse team for their participation and enthusiastic encouragement
Dominique du Peloux, my most faithful reader
Tamara Préaud, Director of the Manufacture de Sèvres archives

Translated from the French by David Wharry

PHOTOGRAPHIC CREDITS
All works reproduced in this book are in the Musée du Louvre
All photographs in this book: Réunion des Musées nationaux (photographs by Daniel Arnaudet, Michèle Bellot, Gérard Blot,
Jean-Gilles Berizzi, Chuzeville, Hervé Lewandowski and Jean Schormans) except pp. 14-15, Giraudon; p.64, Marc Riboud

Editorial and graphic conception: Claire d'HARCOURT
©2001, Éditions du Seuil / Le Funambule
ISBN : 2-02-051643-8
N 51643-1
Dépôt légal : octobre 2001
Loi 49-956 du 16 juillet 1949
sur les publications destinées à la jeunesse

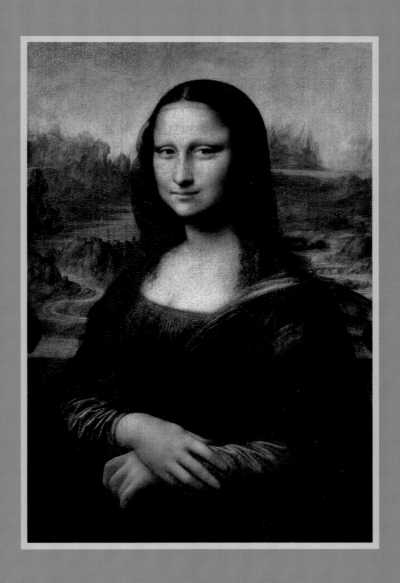

'[…]it seems to me that the Louvre has everything,
that it enables us to love and understand everything,'
wrote the painter Paul Cézanne.
This selection of works from the world's greatest museum
takes you on a journey into the world of art.
Take time to explore each picture, each object,
find all its hidden details.
They are all discussed at the end of the book,
where you can read about the artists' lives
and locate details by lifting the flaps.

Egyptian sarcophagi

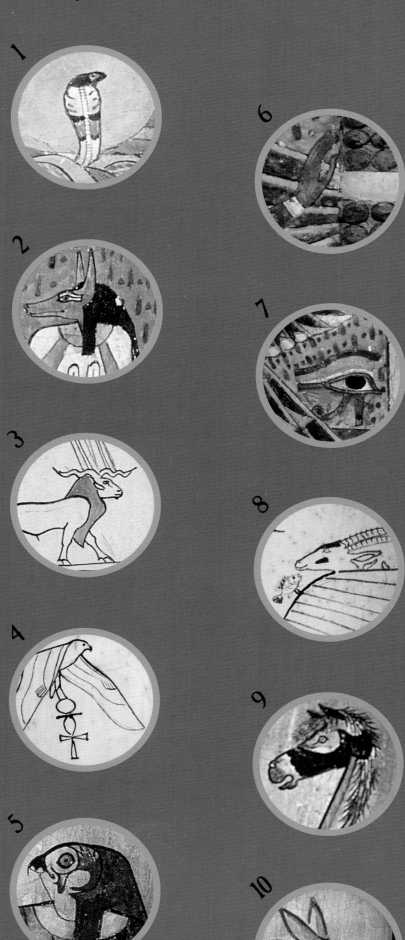

1
2
3
4
5
6
7
8
9
10

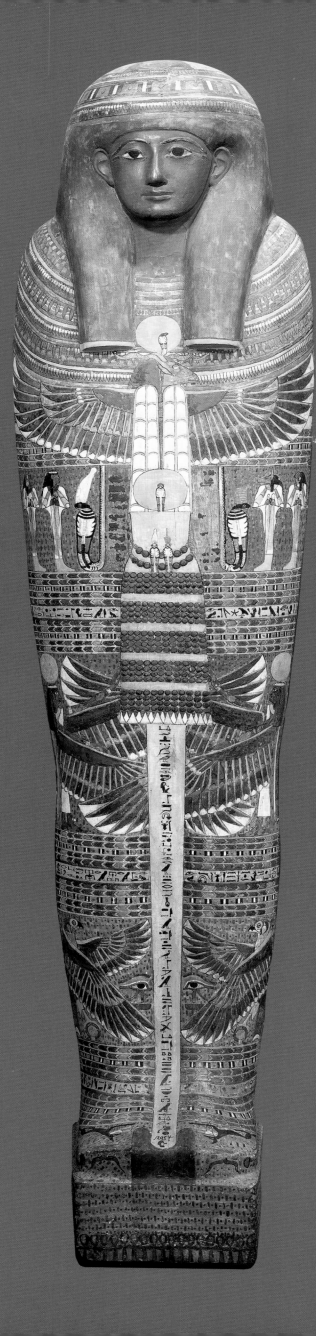

Imeneminet's coffin

1080–664 BC

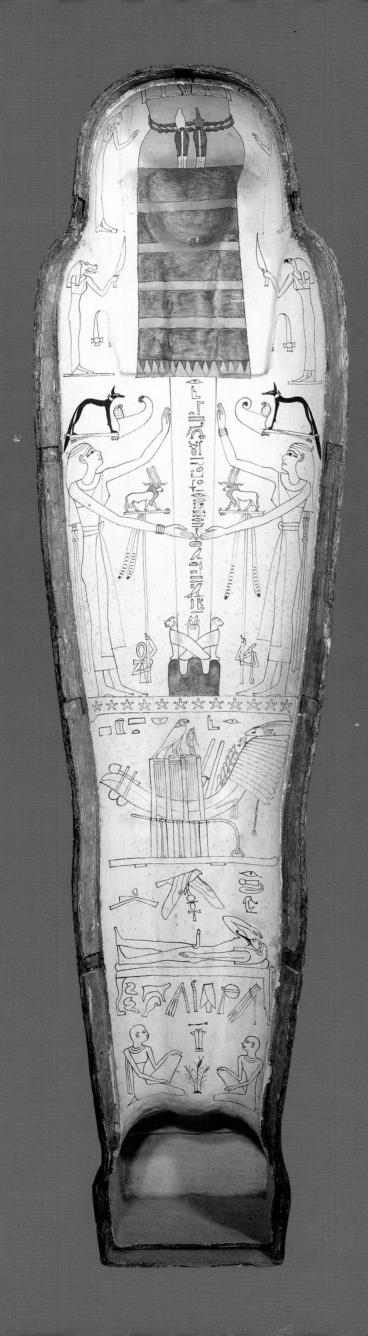
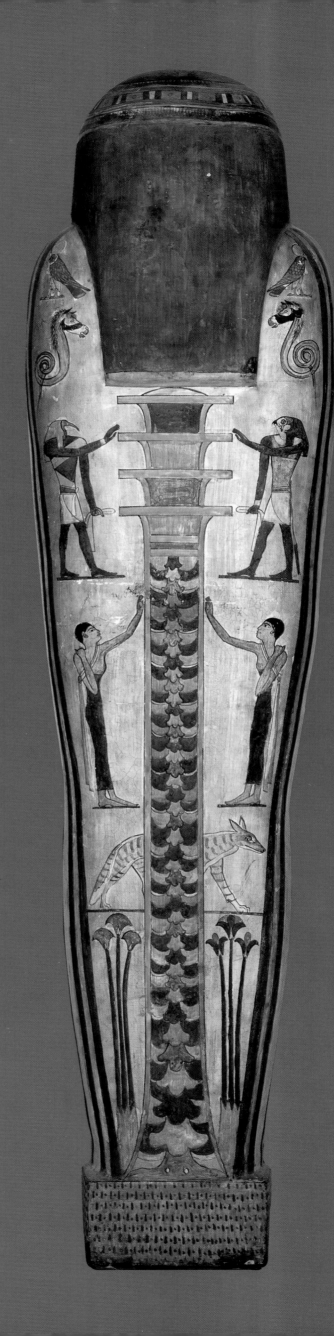

Greek ceramics

Amphora from Milo

circa 400 BC

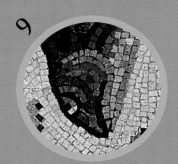

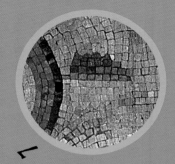

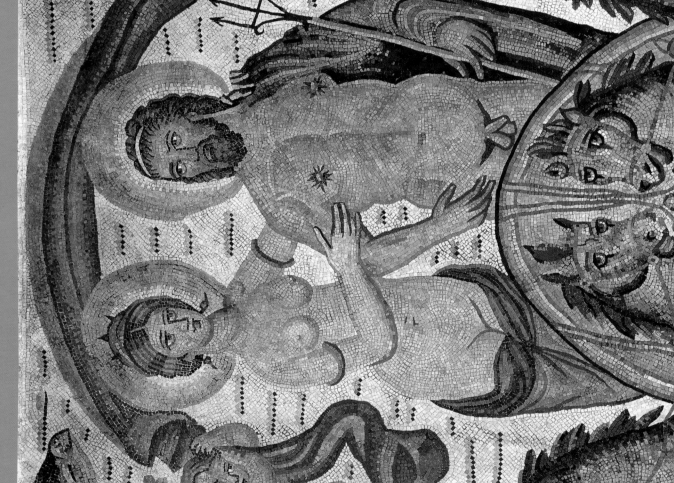

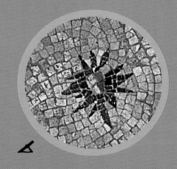

8

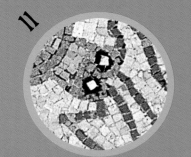

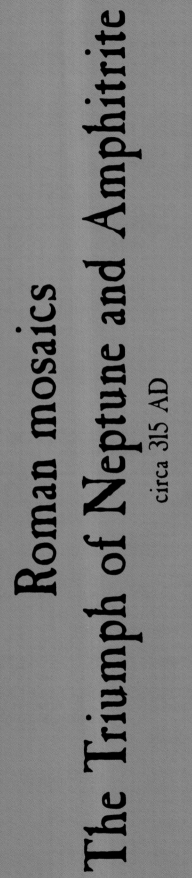

Roman mosaics

The Triumph of Neptune and Amphitrite

circa 315 AD

Gothic stained glass

13th century

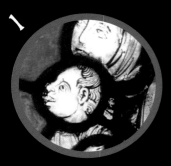

1

2

3

4

5

6

7

8

9

10

Scenes from the story
of Saint Blaise

Scenes from the life
of Saint Nicaise and Saint Eutropie

Fra Angelico
The Coronation of the Virgin circa 1430

1

2

3

4

5

6

7

8

9

10

Jan Van Eyck

The Virgin of Chancellor Rollin

circa 1435

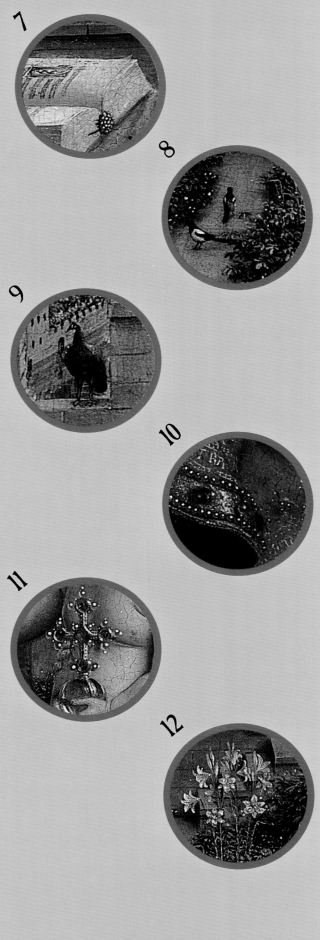

7

8

9

10

11

12

1

2

3

4

Master of the Holy Family

Altarpiece of the Seven Joys of Mary circa 1480

Quentin Metsys

The Banker and his Wife 1514

Lucas van Leyden

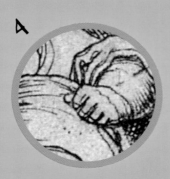

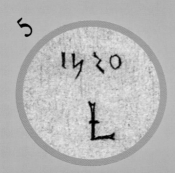

1

2

3

4

5

Two Musicians 1524

6

7

8

Wandering Beggars 1520

Brussels tapestry

Maximilian's Hunts 1533

6

7

8

9

10

Limoges enamel

1

2

3

4

5

6

7

8

9

10

11

12

Plaques of The Aeneid

circa 1530

Hans Sebald Beham

1
2
3
4
5
6
7
8
9
10

Painted table, Scenes from the Life of David

16th century

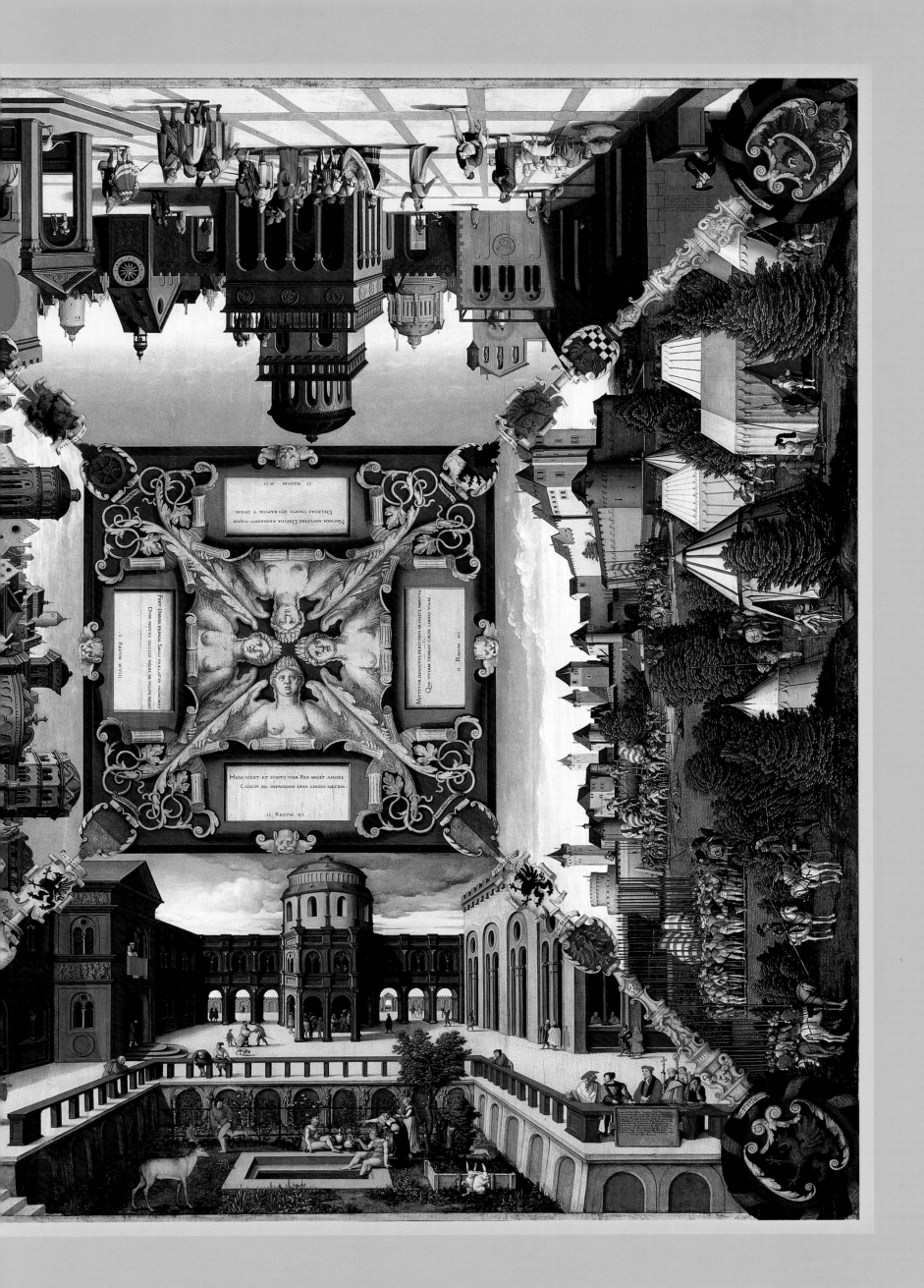

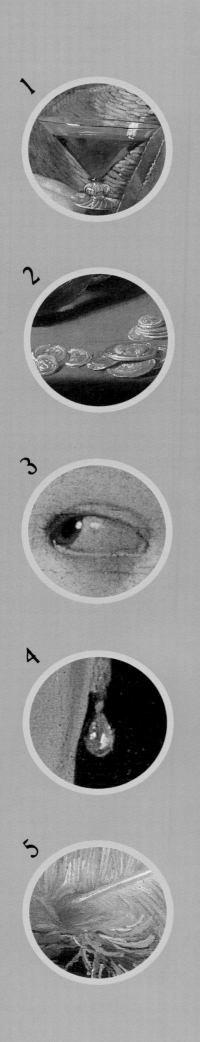

Georges de La Tour

6

7

8

9

10

The Cheat with the Ace of Diamonds circa 1635

1

2

3

4

5

Islamic ceramics, Iran

Scene in a Garden early 17th century

Frans Snyders

1

2

3

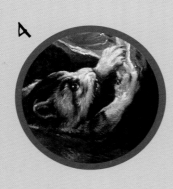

4

The Fishmongers

early 17ᵗʰ century

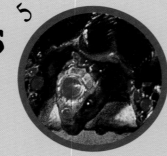

5

6

7

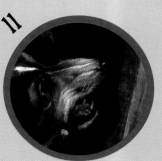

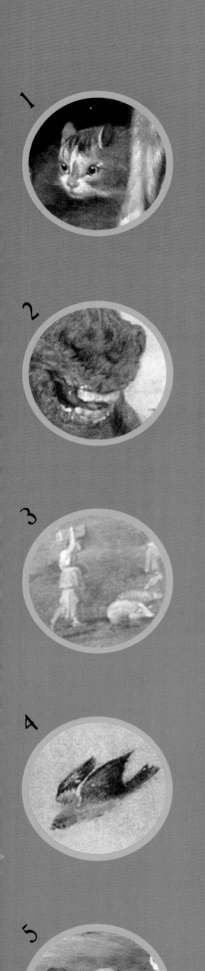

Paul de Vos

Animals Entering
the Ark 17ᵗʰ century

6

7

8

9

10

35

Rembrandt

The Rat-Killer 1632

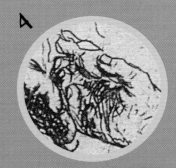

 5
 6
 7
 8

Rembrandt f. 1648.

Beggars Receiving Alms at the Door of a House 1648

Charles André Van Loo

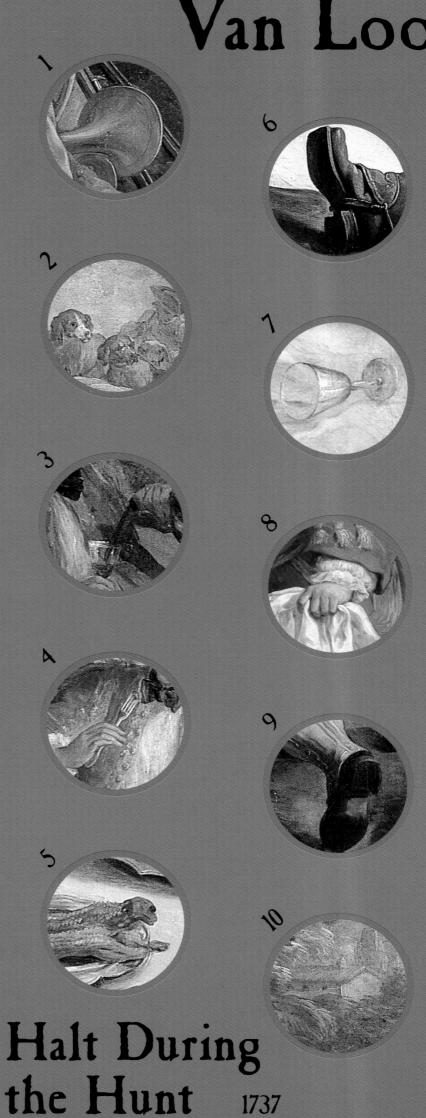

1

6

2

7

3

8

4

9

5

10

Halt During the Hunt 1737

François Boucher

Morning Coffee 1739

1 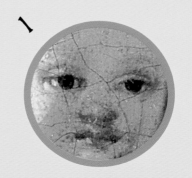 2 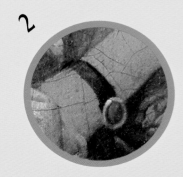 3  4

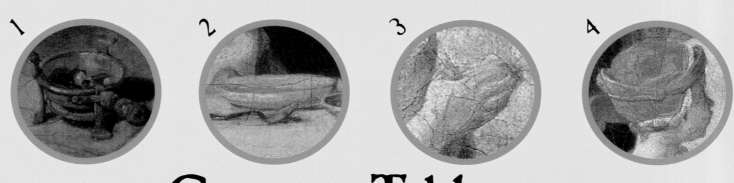

Grace at Table 1740

Jean-Baptiste Siméon Chardin

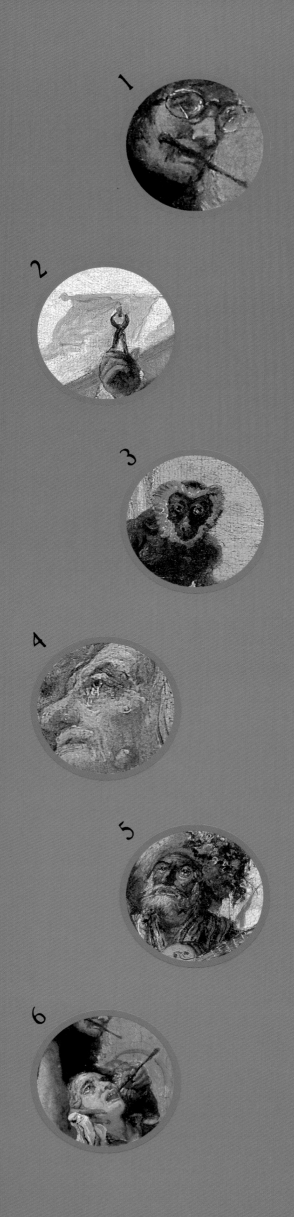

1

2

3

4

5

6

Giandomenico Tiepolo

The Tooth-Puller 1754

Jean-Baptiste Greuze

The Village Bride   1761

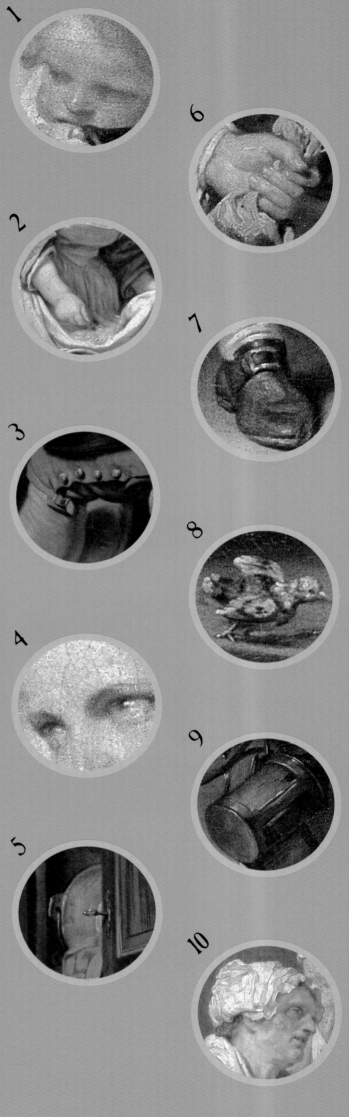

1

2

3

4

5

6

7

8

9

10

Jacques-Louis David

5
6
7
8

The Consecration
of the Emperor Napoleon   1808

hearing

taste

smell

 1

 2

3

4

5

Sèvres porcelain

touch

sight

6

7

8

9

10

The Five Senses Tea Service 1817

1

2

3

4

5

Horace Vernet

6

7

8

9

10

Defending the Barrier at Clichy 1820

A house for eternity: the Egyptian sarcophagus

Sheltered inside his sarcophagus moulding his mummified body like a double, Imeneminet, a high-ranking official responsible for the finances of the Egyptian state nearly three thousand years ago, gazes out at the world of the living with wide-open eyes. Made out of layers of fabric glued together, this was perhaps only the mummy's first, inner casing, to be placed inside a wooden sarcophagus, which in turn might have been encased in a second, outer coffin in the centre of the tomb. Many protective shields and cases were needed for his body to live again in the next world... But it is above all the decor painted on his eternal dwelling place which is the key to Imeneminet's resurrection. A long pillar symbolises the backbone of Osiris, God of the Dead and the Underworld. Murdered then dismembered by his jealous brother, he was resuscitated by wife, Isis, who pieced his body back together again, making the first mummy. Osiris became the protector of the deceased. After judging and weighing their souls, he promises them a new life. The images decorating the coffin or the walls of the tomb are a miniature reproduction of the universe and they obeyed the very strict rules governing sacred art. It was not important that they were beautiful but effective: painted gods, animals, symbols and hieroglyphs provided the dead person with everything he needed in his new existence. The gods' protective wings are wrapped round his body. The boat of the god Sokaris will transport him to the celestial regions. Portrayed with their faces painted green, the colour of resurrection, the gods who reign over the afterlife help him to foil the traps along his journey towards immortality.

Imeneminet's coffin

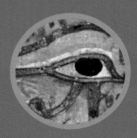

A look at: Ancient Egypt in the Louvre
The *Sarcophagus of Madja*, mummies of cats and crocodiles, The *Seated Scribe*

Greek vases, pictures fired in clay

Amphora from Milo

On this large amphora by the 'Suessula Painter', gods and Giants clash in terrible combat. On one side, in the midst of the fray, Zeus, god of the sky and father of the Greek gods, strikes down a giant who is aiming at Hercules, Zeus's son, armed with a bow. The Winged Victory charges forward on her chariot. The gods' spears and arrows will triumph over the Giants, hairy creatures dressed in animal skins, reputedly invincible, whose bodies ended in serpentine legs. Their gaping mouths, contorted faces and twisted legs express excruciating pain. The painter captured their expressions and movement using the red-figure technique. Up until the 6th century BC, modelled, dried and polished pottery was covered with a clay glaze on which, when it had dried, motifs were painted. During firing the glaze took on a red-orange colour and the motifs went brilliant black due to the chemical properties of the clay used. This was known as the black-figure technique. At the end of the 6th century BC, Greek artists started using the opposite procedure. The composition's background was painted black and the red was reserved for the figures. The artist had new freedom: he could give his figures varied, lifelike expressions and poses. Beforehand, figures had been simply-drawn rigid silhouettes with stiff gestures and poses. Red-figure pottery, with its galloping horses, realistic, muscled bodies, soaring wings and diaphanous drapery, was an entirely different affair. Its delicately-painted scenes overflowed with life. The alchemy of the pottery's firing transformed these everyday vases into magnificent, impervious and durable vessels for wine, water and oil which have lasted down the ages.

A look at: Ancient Greece in the Louvre
The marble *Cyclades Head*, the *Victory of Samothrace*, the *Venus de Milo*

Multicoloured floors: Roman mosaics

The divine couple are riding a chariot drawn by four whinnying, rearing horses whose lower, snake-shaped bodies are emerging from the waters. Neptune, god of the sea, blue haired and bearded, tufts of seaweed on his chest, holds his emblem, the trident, the weapon of tuna fishermen. At his side, arm round his shoulders, his wife Amphitrite is decked with bracelets, ear rings and a diadem. Cupids are fishing from two boats whilst others, resting on dolphins, swim amongst the fish, octopuses, cuttlefish and shells. The seawater is represented by lines drawn in light blue and black cubes. This is not a painting but a mosaic, a picture composed of thousands of small marble limestone and glass cubes of sparkling colour. The glass cubes enable a wide range of colours and reflect the light.

This panel once decorated the floor of a salon of a wealthy villa in Constantine, a Roman colony in Africa. Unlike a picture, which can be seen all at once, a mosaic reveals itself gradually as one advances into a room. Because the spectator does not have an overall view, the mosaic doesn't obey the same compositional rules: the figures are arranged vertically, above one another. The floors, but also the walls and ceilings of Roman villas were decorated with mosaics. Contrary to packed earth, mosaic is a hard-wearing, washable, practical and comfortable interior decoration. It was in Roman times that mosaic developed into a major art form.

The Triumph of Neptune and Amphitrite

A look at: the Etruscan and Roman eras in the Louvre
The *Sarcophagus of the Spouses*, the *Cupids and Dolphins* mosaic, the *Goblet with Skeletons* from Boscoreale

Jigsaw puzzles of light: stained glass in the Middle Ages

These 'comic strips' in coloured glass are read from top to bottom. The medallions recount the lives of the saints to the faithful, most of whom couldn't read: the trial of Saint Nicaise, bishop of Reims, his martydom and that of his sister, Saint Eutrope, by Vandal soldiers in chain mail; Saint Blaise's miraculous saving of a baby, choking to death on a fishbone, and her healing of a woman. In the 13th century, cathedrals, with their stone lacework and spires soared into the sky. The thick walls of Romanesque churches were pierced with windows. Gothic cathedrals, gigantic edifices of stone and glass, were decorated with large stained glass windows. Sparkling like precious stones, they inundated church interiors with a diffuse light, creating a dreamlike atmosphere conducive to prayer. On panes of glass coloured with metal oxides — powders which, depending on the temperature, produced glass of different colour — backgrounds and figures were painted in *grisaille*, a mixture of glass powder and copper powder mixed with wine or urine, which the heat vitrified to the glass. Drapery and gestures were drawn in flowing, natural lines. The final stage in the production of stained glass windows, an art which reached its height in the 13th century, was the assembly of these pieces of painted glass using strips of lead.

A look at: the Middle Ages in the Louvre
The emperor Charlemagne's coronation crown and sword, the 'Baptistery of Saint Louis', the Maastricht Binding-Case

Scenes from the story of Saint Blaise

Scenes from the life of Saint Nicaise and Saint Eutropie

Space and depth: the march towards the Renaissance

A flight of multicoloured marble steps lead up to Heaven and the throne of Christ, who is about to place a gold crown incrusted with gemstones and pearls on the head of his kneeling mother, the Virgin Mary. In the blinding light of the sky, a celestial host of monks, saints and angels playing instruments watch the crowning of the queen of the heavens. The names of some of the saints are written on their halos, others are recognisable by characteristic attributes: Saint Louis' fleur-de-lis crown, Saint Madeleine's vase, which she used to wash Jesus' feet, the wheel on which Saint Catherine was martyred, Saint Agnes' lamb, the knife of Saint Bartholomew, who was skinned alive. The altarpiece was placed in full view of the congregation above the altar of a convent church in Florence. The use of gold leaf and bright primary colours and the delicate portrayal of the faces recall the illuminations of the late Middle Ages, however the picture's expert composition is inspired by the discoveries of the dawning Italian Renaissance. The pyramidal composition shows surprising new mastery of space. The geometric perspective of the tiles and steps gives the work depth. Each figure — there are around sixty — is firmly rooted in this three dimensional world: seen from head to foot in the foreground, only half visible in the mid-distance, only the heads of the saints and angels visible in the background. Successive planes converging on Heaven, which seems to be infinitely far away.

The Coronation of the Virgin

A look at:
15th-century Italy in the Louvre
The Battle of San Romano by Paolo Uccello,
Portrait of an Old Man with a Young Boy by Domenico Ghirlandaio

The magic of oils 15th – century Flemish painting

Chancellor Philippe le Bon, Duke of Burgundy, is received by the Virgin Mary and blessed by the Infant Jesus. Chancellor Rolin bestowed this honour upon himself by having himself painted, as was customary, as the donator of the picture he had commissioned for a church. Nevertheless, the painter Jan Van Eyck painted a pitilessly accurate portrait of this illustrious, yet hard and unscrupulous figure of the royal court, even showing the veins standing out on his temple. It is thanks to the use of oil paint — he had the revolutionary idea of using oil to bind his colour powders — that he can render the minutiae of reality in such detail, with such brilliance and depth, by superimposing semi-transparent layers of fluid paint known as glazes. The arcade opens onto a landscape, a genuine 'picture within a picture' in which the eye can wander. The people walking or riding over the bridge or through the streets of the town are less than a millimetre high. The progressive gradation of tones, the diminishing scale of the figures and objects and the perspective of the floor tiles create the illusion of distance. Van Eyck sought to capture the light and space of reality. But for him, and other Flemish artists of his time, God is present in all visible things. Each realistic detail of everyday life has a symbolic and Biblical meaning. The Angel's wings reflect the colours of the rainbow, symbol of the alliance between God and man. The two banks of the river represent the celestial world on the Virgin Mary's side and the earthly world on the Chancellor's side. And the bridge linking the two banks represents the prayer which can link man to God. The picture scintillates with oil paint's sparkling colours, such as the famous 'Van Eyck red' of the Virgin's sumptuous robe.

The Virgin of Chancellor Rollin

A look at:
The Flemish Primitives in the Louvre
The Annunciation triptych by Rogier Van der Weyden,
The Ressurrection triptych by Hans Memling

Folding paintings: the window behind the altar

On Sundays and festival days, the shutters of the altarpieces on church altars were opened to reveal to the stunned congregation the gold leaf and sparkling colours inside. During the week, the panels of these articulated paintings remained shut, with only their duller exterior panels visible. The opening and closing of these polyptychs (from the Greek word meaning 'with several folds') was an important weekly event but it also had another, more practical purpose, that of protecting the precious materials with which the interior pictures were painted from the damp. This is why in the hot, dry countries of Europe such as Italy, altarpieces are often made out of a single panel of wood, like those of Fra Angelico, whereas in the Low Countries or in Germany paintings had to be protected by shutters. In the rich and prosperous city of Cologne, an important art centre in 15th-century Germany, the 'Master of the Holy Family' designed his altarpiece, made out of oak panels on hinges, as a huge window opening onto scenes from the life of the Virgin Mary, illuminated by a magnificent gold ground. Divided into three episodes — 'The Adoration of the Magi', 'The Presentation in the Temple' and 'The Apparition of Christ to Mary' — this was the centre panel of the large *Altarpiece of the Seven Joys of Mary*. The four other 'joys' are on panels which are separate today. To depict the sacred was the sole aim of the artist who painted this work teeming with angels. Yet he chooses to realistically represent details and facial expressions: Joseph's pained look, for instance, as he delves into his purse for money for the offering…

A look at:
altarpieces in the Louvre
The *Altarpiece of the 'Parlement de Paris'*, the *Antwerp Triptych*, the *Sedano Triptych*

Altarpiece of the Seven Joys of Mary

Reflections in a mirror: the symbolism of everyday life

With an attentiveness dictated perhaps by greed, the banker painstakingly weighs gold coins in his shop. Coins, pearls, rings and other precious objects are strewn over the table in front of him. Either distracted or fascinated by these riches, his wife has looked up from her illuminated prayer book. Their left hands are both poised over the table, his weighing a gold coin on the scales, hers turning the page of the book, revealing a miniature of a Madonna and Child: two worlds in opposition, the material and the spiritual. One shouldn't forget that Antwerp, where the painter lived, was a great artistic centre but also the richest trading city in Europe. The moral of Quentin Metsys' painting, that one mustn't allow oneself to be distracted from prayer by worldly goods, is emphasised by the scales, a symbol of justice evoking the Last Judgement. The smooth, glossy oil paint renders the most microscopic details: the hand-written letters in the book, the painter's signature on a parchment on the shelf, the coins, all different, the softness of a fur collar. Metsys paints everyday objects with such technical mastery they seem real. The artist is particularly interested in shiny things which catch the light: pearls and a glass vase, silverware and reflections in a mirror. The latter reveals a part of the room one cannot see in the picture, where the painter is, and the landscape outside. Quentin Metsys magically uses the mirror and the open door, through which we can see two people chatting, to construct a space seen from different viewpoints. He brings the vast and distant outside world into the closed world of the shop, giving it surprising depth.

A look at: European painting in the 16th century
The Ship of Fools by Hieronymus Boschi, the *Mona Lisa* by Leonardo da Vinci, *The Marriage at Cana* by Veronese

The Banker and his Wife

Multiple images: the revolution of engraving

Bent over his sheet of copper, Lucas van Leyden gripped the handle of his burin and with its metal blade gouged a groove outlining the hooked chin of an old woman. Little by little, the drawing appeared in negative and the wrong way round in the copper: a man sitting under a tree playing the lute, accompanied by his wife on the viol. The engraver then inked the plate and wiped it so that ink remained only in the grooves. Then, when paper was pressed against it in a press the drawing was printed the right way round, and could subsequently be printed as many times as the artist wanted. Engraving in copper, derived from the silversmith's art, was called line engraving. This technique, developed in the 15th century, of which Lucas van Leyden and Albrecht Durer were great masters, was preceded several years earlier by wood engraving, in which the drawing wasn't gouged into the wood block but cut away in relief instead. Xylography, another name for the woodcut, was a popular art form at a time when the printed book didn't yet exist. Line engraving, however, whose print runs were much more limited, was reserved for the elite. The hollow grooves of line engravings are gouged out with a burin or by using acid, as in this drawing swarming with impish little children carried along by a couple of beggars, on their backs in baskets or on a donkey. Lucas van Leyden's engravings, very sought after, were snapped up at fairs all over Northern Europe.

Two Musicians · Wandering Beggars

A look at: graphic arts in the Louvre
View of the Arco Valley by Albrecht Durer,
Two Saddled Horses by Pisanello,
The Witches by Hieronymus Bosch

Paintings woven out of wool, silk, gold and silver

A horseman brandishing a hunting sword is about to confront an enormous wild boar, furiously standing its ground. A dog is already lying wounded and others are attacking the beast, one of them protected by a padded coat. This brave hunter is probably the Hapsburg Emperor Ferdinand I and not his grandfather Miximilian I as previously thought. This December scene is part of an impressive series of twelve tapestries, a giant encyclopaedia of deer and wild boar hunting, considered to be the greatest masterpiece of the art of tapestry. It took nearly a year for five people to weave just one of these wall hangings. To faithfully reproduce all the nuances of the painter's drawing, from a full-scale cartoon which they had to copy, the tapestry weavers, called heddle setters, used wool died in refined colours and other extremely delicate materials (silk, silver and gold thread). Colours are used in flat areas or blended in hatching using alternating threads of different tones and drawing, volume, modelling and gradation are rendered with the utmost subtlety. The depths of the forest into which the hunters have penetrated could almost be painted. Against the increasingly distant planes of the background, the agitation of the figures, the vegetation, every blade of grass, even the fur and coats of the animals, whose hairs we can almost distinguish, are as realistic as the most detailed painting. At the beginning of the 16th century, production in the Brussels workshops where the *Maximilian's Hunts* series was woven surpassed in quality and output that of all other great tapestry centres.

A look at:
tapestries in the Louvre
The Hunters' Meal, The Story of Scipio,
The Elephant Tapestry

Maximilian's Hunts

As brilliant as precious stones: Limoges enamel

After a ten-year siege, the Greeks took Troy by managing to trick the Trojans into taking a gigantic wooden horse into the city. The soldiers hidden inside the horse then jumped out, opened the gates and set Troy on fire. In the books of *The Aeneid* , the Roman poet Virgil recounts the adventures of Aeneas, a Trojan prince who fled the burning city aided by Aeolus, the god of wind, who blew his ships towards foreign lands. How did the master who illustrated Aeneas' trials and tribulations on these enamelled plaques obtain such brilliant colours? Enamel is a kind of glass coloured by metallic oxides: tin for the opaque white, cobalt for blue, manganese for violet, antimony for yellow, etc. In the Middle Ages, enamel was usually chased: the enamel powder was laid in cavities gouged in the metal with a burin, into which the touches of colour were set like precious stones. At the end of the 15th century, a new technique, painted enamel, was developed in Limoges, France. Using a spatula, the artist spreads on to the copper plaque successive layers of a paste made of metallic oxides bound with oils. One after the other, these layers are fired in a kiln: the first, transparent, is to protect the copper ground; the drawing is then transposed on to

the second, white coating; the coloured layers are then applied and successively fired according to the various enamels' resistance to heat. Heated to melting point, the enamel liquefies, and when it cools, hardens again, bonding itself to the metal. To catch the light, the artist placed transparent enamel on thin strips of silver. Unlike paint, the brightness and brilliance of enamel colours lasts for centuries.

A look at: enamel in the Louvre
The Pair of mirror discs belonging to Louis d'Anjou, *The Reliquary of the Massacre of the Innocent*, the helmet of Charles IX by Pierre Redon

Plaques of The Aeneid

Meticulous detail and fantasy: the German Renaissance

Painted table:
Scenes from the Life of David

A look at:
the German Renaissance in the Louvre
Self-Portrait by Albrecht Durer, *Erasmus* by Hans Holbein, the sculpture of *Saint Mary Magdalene* by Gregor Erhart

To take in the whole picture, you have to walk around it and look at it from all sides. Because in fact it isn't a picture at all but a table top, divided into four triangular panels depicting different episodes in David's life, from the Bible. In the first, women are coming out of Jerusalem to meet King Saul and David, who has killed Goliath. In the second, Bathsheba is bathing, lusted after by David. To the right we can see the portrait of the Cardinal of Brandenburg, the man who commissioned this work and one of the most important figures in early 16th-century Germany. In the third, Uriah, Bathsheba's husband, is laying siege to the town of Rabbath, where he sent David to get rid of him. The fourth scene shows the prophet Nathan rebuking David for his sin, who repents, and illustrates the parable of the rich man who steals the poor man's lamb. The artist has portrayed himself as the poor man holding a lamb in his arms to Nathan's left. The classical squares and Renaissance towns Hans Sebald Beham chose to structure these compositions are imaginary. Swarming with details, the scenes are painted in bright colours with the finesse of a miniaturist and a blend of fantasy and realism inherited from the Middle Ages. Beham's drawing is as precise and sharp as the incisive furrows of the burin he used in his work as an engraver. After Durer, he belongs to the generation of original and unclassifiable artists of the German Renaissance.

Looks and gestures: painting the human mind

The atmosphere is stifling and time has come to a standstill in this cramped, enclosed space lit only by a cold pale light. The faces are tense and the silence is oppressive. We are witnessing something happening in secret: we have to guess what by deciphering the expressions and body language of the protagonists. Only the spectator can see the cheat pulling out the game-winning card, the ace of diamonds, hidden in his belt. The two women are his accomplices judging from their sideways looks and the signs they are making to each other. The rich young man, his elegance emphasised by the bright colours and fine material of his clothes, is fooled by their ploy. Absorbed in the card game, he is about to play and lose. The tension is electric, especially since, when this picture was painted at the beginning of the 17th century, gambling was forbidden by the Church. The players were running the risk of being excommunicated and cheats were sentenced to the galleys. The tension is compounded by the fact that the painting is not just describing visible reality. It is also a parable. Like the prodigal son in the Bible, the naive and unsuspecting young man, surrounded by the temptations of gambling, wine and women, is not only

going to lose the game and the gold coins on the table but also himself. The dirty fingernails of these elegant but badly groomed characters, emphasise their moral impurity. In 17th-century France, a new style of painting emerged known as 'genre painting', which depicted everyday scenes painted from nature. Caravaggio, an Italian painter who greatly influenced La Tour, was one of the masters of this movement, known as 'Caravaggism'. He invented these scenes in which ordinary people are frozen in mid-action, seen close up and lit by bright, contrasted light which makes their vivid colours stand out against a dark background.

The Cheat with the Ace of Diamonds

A look at:
card players in the Louvre
The Fortune-Teller by Lucas van Leyden,
Interior of a Cabaret by David Teniers the Younger,
Cabaret Scene by Louis Léopold Boilly

Paradise in a garden: Islam or the art of decoration

Scene in a Garden

Kneeling in the middle of a wonderful garden with trees in bloom, two young men are reading poems. A third man, standing, is listening to them. A woman is bringing them a large jar of sweets which she will place on the ground next to the tray of fruit and the bottle of drink. Harmony reigns in this unreal and magical paradise. The garden is very important in Islamic civilisation. With its luxurious vegetation, it represents Heaven, the 'sublime garden' promised by the Koran. It is a key theme in numerous Persian miniatures and **objets d'art**. In *Scene in a Garden* there is no

concern with space, perspective effects, modelling or light and shade. Contrary to western painting during the same period, the illusion of reality is not important. The leaves on the trees, flowers and grass are not intended to look real. All that counts is the formal beauty of these motifs, which are repeated and juxtaposed like the notes of some fluid rhythmic music. The brightly-coloured forms which cover the entire panel stand out against the white enamel background. There is no sky, no empty space. Wherever one looks, there are pleasing sights. Drawn in sinuous curves, the graceful looking figures in their elegant flowered robes seem to blend into the surrounding vegetation, which is like a carpet of flowers and colours. Like the trees, stones and grass, the people are ornaments, arabesques (Arab ornamental motifs with stylised forms).

These painted ceramic panels adorned the walls of luxurious Iranian palaces like sumptuous tapestries. Islamic art always has a practical function, that of decorating and transforming everyday things such as the walls of houses, mosques and palaces but also books, crockery and furniture.

A look at:
oriental antiquities in the Louvre
The *Winged Bulls of Khorsabad*,
the *Archers of the Guard of Darius*, the *Mantes Carpet*

Fish, fowl, flowers and fruit: the still life

On market day in Antwerp, fishmongers are setting out the fish, brought from the port in the background, on their stall: slithery eels, salmon, skate, crayfish, crabs and octopuses still quivering, or fish already stiff and glassy-eyed, their mouths wide open. Surprisingly, there are also seals and turtles in the foreground, overflowing off the stall onto the ground, as if trying to burst out of the canvas. We are riveted by their sheer presence, by the magical skill with which Snyders has painted these creatures' viscous, gleaming forms and the iridescent tints of their scales. We can almost smell the salt. On huge canvases over two metres high and three and a half metres wide, Snyders painted a series of four stalls (fish, game, fruit and vegetables), the largest group of still lifes in existence and perhaps the largest ever executed. Then, for years, he painted variations and replicas of these masterpieces — such as *The Fishmongers* —, now in Saint Petersburg. These fish and sea creatures are like a catalogue of models, from which the artist later repeatedly drew. In the 17th century in Flanders and Holland a new genre of painting was developed known as the 'still life', whose central subject matter was inanimate objects. However, in

Snyders' still lifes, the picture is 'inhabited', not only by people in the background but by intruders such as the cat stealing a piece of salmon. His kitchens, market stalls, fruit and banquets show the abundant wealth in the Low Countries during that period. They are also a vibrant tribute to God, who created these marvels for our delight and nourishment. The scale and spirit of Snyders' compositions make him the inventor of the Flemish baroque still life.

A look at:
still lifes in the Louvre
Spring, Summer, Autumn and Winter by Arcimboldo,
A Dessert by Jan Davidz de Heem, *The Skate* by Chardin

The Fishmongers

The triumph of nature: animal painting

Animals Entering the Ark

A lion and lioness, a ewe and ram, a hen and cock, each couple patiently awaiting their turn to embark upon the huge ark that Noah built on God's orders. In doing so they will escape the Deluge with which the Creator is going to punish man for his disobedience. The animals overflow from the cramped composition Paul de Vos chose for this biblical scene, which gives the impression that only part of the scene has been depicted. Almost at the same time as the still life appeared in the 17th century, a rather similar genre, the animal painting, developed, in

which Snyders also excelled. Human beings are absent or merely sketched in the background, as in Paul de Vos' painting. Noah's Ark and the Garden of Eden were the biblical themes most often chosen by these painters since they were pretexts for painting a kind of pictorial encyclopaedia of the animal kingdom. This trend in painting also had its roots in a wider movement advocating a return to nature, in which animals were attributed qualities superior to man's because they live simply and obey the laws of nature. The horse dominates this composition, his tall outline standing out theatrically against the sky. The horse was the animal most often represented by draughtsmen and painters, ever since Leonardo da Vinci had painstakingly studied its proportions and anatomy. Animal painting shows the new scientific interest in the physical and physiological. Paul de Vos may have been inspired by the illustrated plates in natural history books, by dead or stuffed animals or by his visits to the zoo in Antwerp, where numerous artists of his day went to draw from life.

A look at:
animals in the Louvre
The Garden of Eden by Jan Breugel,
Animals Entering the Ark by Bassano

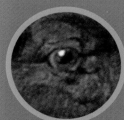

The acid bite of etching

On a copper plate coated with varnish, using a pointed tool, Rembrandt drew a rat-killer proposing his services to a villager on his doorstep. On the end of a pole, the man is carrying a cage, to prove the effectiveness of his poison, full of live rats and festooned with dead ones. Several years later, on another copper plate, he engraved *Beggars Receiving Alms at the Door of a House*, the composition of which looks as if it were drawn from life and is similar: another villager at his door, another old man with a beard giving alms to beggars. The pointed tool incises the varnish, exposing the copper beneath. The plate is then dipped in a bath of acid known as *eau-forte* which eats into the exposed copper. As in the grooves made by the engraver's burin, the ink will only lodge in the hollow lines, which are printed on the sheet of paper pressed to the plate. After printing the first proofs, Rembrandt often corrected or modified his engraving, working directly on the copper plate using the hard needle (known as a 'dry point') or a burin. Drawing lines into the metal with a sure hand, he added shadows, accentuated certain grooves or scratched to get rid of a detail, creating a different 'state' and another, different work. But

A look at: Rembrandt in the Louvre
*Holy Family, Self-Portrait at the Easel,
Philosopher in Meditation*

Rembrandt wasn't merely a highly-skilled craftsman. No artist has painted ordinary people, the poor and abandoned, with such compassion and passion. His works exude profound emotion and great humanity. A sublime portraitist in both his paintings and drawings, he was a keen and astute observer of human sentiment and the human face, which he drew with great power, accuracy and sensitivity. He exploited all the expressive possibilities of the eau-forte, whose free-flowing technique accentuates the hand's slightest hesitation. Scratching and hatching create the play of shadow and light in these vibrant scenes from Rembrandt's life.

The Rat-Killer   Beggars Receiving Alms
at the Door of a House

18ᵗʰ – century painting or the art of decoration

Halt During the Hunt

**A look at:
hunt meals in the Louvre**
The Hunt Meal by Jean François de Troy,
Meal After the Hunt by Nicolas Lancret

How refined this pastoral meal is, what urbane behaviour, what elegant dress, what an atmosphere of luxury and pleasure... Fine food and wines have been set out on the immaculate white damask tablecloth. Yet it is supposed to be just a simple picnic during a day out hunting, an everyday scene of aristocratic life. Lords and valets are eagerly serving noble ladies, nothing has been forgotten, even the mule decked with plumes carrying the food. But who are the elegant people gathered here? It has been suggested that Louis XV is one of them, surrounded by three sisters who were his mistresses — the picture was painted to decorate the royal apartments in the château at Fontainebleau, the king's hunting lodge, which Van Loo and the greatest artists of the time were commissioned to decorate. In the 18ᵗʰ century, a new taste for comfort and the intimacy of smaller rooms, each with their use — dining room, boudoir, etc. — modified the residences of the aristocracy and the court. In these private apartments, the interior decoration changed, like clothes, with the whims of fashion. The amorous, frivolous and refined scenes of the paintings were as integral a part of the overall harmony as were the furniture and wall hangings. Van Loo's *Halt During the Hunt* was one of a group of canvases intended, like the numerous mirrors, to be set in the white and gold sculpted panelling of the king's large dining room. Conceived on the scale of the room, as part of its setting, the painting's function is to decorate and please the eye.

Everyday moments of happiness: painting intimacy

Morning Coffee   Grace at Table

In a clean, plain room with a tiled floor, a dignified and moderately well-to-do woman makes her children say grace before serving the steaming soup: the everyday poetry and gestures of a simple, happy and peaceful life, the loving, silent concern of a hard-working dutiful mother. Then, a completely different world: a brightly-lit Parisian drawing room with its luxurious gilded rococo mouldings, in which two rich, elegant women with their children are being served coffee — a very fashionable luxury which had just been introduced in France. Apparently, these two contemporary canvases have very different subjects and treatment. One has subdued tones applied in thick impasto, in which the greys and browns stand out on the white tablecloth, the other has a rich, light palette and the fluid paint brings out the mother-of-pearl complexions. Yet these two pictures have several things in common, the first being the intimacy of the family scenes they depict. Inspired by the Dutch, French painters had begun taking an interest in private and family life, illustrating the new interest in the individual in 18th-century society. These snapshots of daily life capture a moment, its exchanges of looks and frozen gestures. Like Chardin, François Boucher wanted to paint a simple moment of happiness (this may even have been his own family), and both of them placed children at the heart of their pictures. Another similarity is the two children seen frontally, one looking at us, as if to draw us into the painting. There is also the striking similarity of the poses of the two children in profile, sitting on their tiny chairs. The two painters illustrate the growing interest at that time in childhood and education. The toys that were beginning to be manufactured then — the little drum in Chardin's picture, the doll and horse in Boucher's — are examples of this.

A look at: children in the Louvre
The Young Beggar by Murillo,
Family of Peasants in an Interior by the Le Nain brothers,
the busts of Louise Brongniart by Jean-Antoine Houdon

Buffoons and charlatans: Venetian comedy

The Tooth-Puller

A look at:
tooth-pullers in the Louvre
The Tooth-Puller by Gerrit Van Honthorst,
The Tooth-Puller by Gerard Dou

In a street, a man standing on a platform is brandishing a tooth held with pincers. This charlatan with his monkey, sign and acolyte operating next to him, is a tooth-puller, or dentist of his time. The boisterous crowd milling round him is a mixture of contrasting figures: a Punchinello with his large white hat and hooked nose, a busker, a cake seller, an old woman and several elegant aristocrats. Many among them are masked, illustrating Giandomenico Tiepolo's particular interest in festivals and carnivals. In the 18th century, Venice was a city of festivities and pleasure in which the carnival was all-important. The carnival disguises and masques were inspired by the Commedia del'Arte, a genre of Italian popular theatre which developed in the 16th century and is still performed today. Whether masked or not, the faces in *The Tooth-Puller* are painted with an acute sense of observation and caricature. We are watching a spectacle, treated theatrically with bright colours. Its carefree and gay atmosphere reflects the spirit of the period, which Tiepolo tried to capture with tongue-in-cheek irony and sometimes dark humour. These picturesque and satirical scenes from daily life are not completely representative of 18th-century Venetian painting, however, which was also characterised by its grandiose interiors and panoramic townscapes (the *vedute*), which became the speciality of painters such as Guardi.

The painting of fine feelings: the moralist art of Greuze

The Village Bride

A look at:
French painting in the 18th century in the Louvre
Portrait of Louis XIV by Hyacinthe Rigaud,
The Bolt by Honoré Fragonard,
Pierrot by Jean-Antoine Watteau

Surrounded by his family, a father gives his son-in-law to be the purse containing his daughter's dowry. A peasant household is the setting for this theatrical scene with a light, ordered composition. The wedding ceremony has brought the family together, and of course the notary, who is studying the marriage contract. Each person's expression and pose expresses different feelings, which the artist has tellingly conveyed: the sadness of the young sister who is losing a companion, the jealousy of the elder brother who wasn't chosen, the shy tenderness of the bride-to-be, the curiosity of the little brother standing on tiptoes to get a better look, the loving mother and the dignity of the father making his recommendations. The hen with her chicks pecking at grain thrown to them by the little girl provides a picturesque and poetic note by drawing a parallel between the human and animal world. The aim of Greuze's realistic and enlightening pictures of social customs was to arouse emotions and fine feelings. They were criticised by those who found his pathos exaggerated and unconvincing, but they reflect the moralising tendencies in painting at that time. Bought by Louis XVI, *The Village Bride* marked the peak of Greuze's career. The philosopher Diderot went into raptures upon seeing an artist finally contriving 'to move us, instruct us, correct us and incite us to virtue'. After the brilliant paintings of a courtly and frivolous society by 18th-century artists who preceded Greuze, the return to a moral, serious art reflected the spirit of the times.

Grandiose testimonies: history painting

The occasion is a solemn one: all eyes are on the crown that the Emperor Napoleon the Ist is augustly holding up before placing it on the head of his wife, Josephine, kneeling on the altar steps. Examine the faces of this fascinating gallery of very realistic and sometimes caricatured life-size portraits. Some one hundred and fifty people. Apart from the Pope, unenthusiastically bestowing his blessing on the scene, one can recognise, in the background on the left, Napoleon's brothers and sisters, on the right, the principal dignitaries of the Empire and, in the gallery behind, his mother, who was against the marriage and did not attend at the real-life event. David was ordered to make this 'alteration' by the Emperor himself, who liked to get his own way. In a box above, the painter has included himself, sketching the scene from life. It could obviously only have been a sketch for this gigantic picture, more than sixty square metres, which took him over three years to paint after having had the principal figures of this impressive assembly pose at length for him in his studio. He demonstrates here his great talent for portraiture, painstaking attention to the slightest detail and acute sense of the theatrical. Beneath the enormous vaults of the cathedral, the crowd surrounds the imperial couple, whose long ermine-trimmed velvet robes stand out sumptuously. Napoleon himself commissioned this painting. Intent on showing his power and handing down a grandiose picture of it to posterity, he personally supervised its execution to ensure that every detail glorified him. He is reported to have praised David by declaring, 'What relief, what truth! This isn't a painting, one can walk into the picture!'

A look at:
David in the Louvre
The Death of Marat, The Oath of the Horatii, Madame Récamier

The Consecration of the Emperor Napoleon

Miniature pictures: Sèvres porcelain

At her mother's side, a little girl marvels at a display of butterflies and stuffed birds; in a picture-dealer's shop, walls covered with paintings; different-coloured plaques in the entrance of an ironmonger's shop; a rainbow standing out against a dark sky... With the talent of a miniaturist, Jean-Charles Develly painted every detail of these scenes evoking sight on the curved surface of a teapot. One of the five senses is illustrated on each of the service's pieces: sight, touch, hearing, smell and taste. One can even make out gherkins in the jars in the tiny picture on the cup devoted to taste. The light, sparkling colour of these images stands out against the green background colour and gold decoration. This service is made of hard-paste porcelain, a kaolin (a pure, white clay) based-substance which produces delicate, translucent ceramics which are resistant to knocks and scratches. The secret of this technique, jealously kept by Chinese emperors since the 4th century, intrigued European potters and alchemists for centuries. It wasn't until the end of the 18th century, shortly before the Five Senses Tea Service was made, that France discovered kaolin and the first hard-paste porcelain came out of the kilns of the royal manufactory at Sèvres. Once each piece has been fired — at this stage it is called a *biscuit* — it is painted with enamel and precious metals, then refired to vitrify the colours and metals in the enamel. The Manufacture de Sèvres made numerous services used at court and gifts offered by the King to French and foreign personalities. The *Five Senses Tea Service* was commissioned by Louis XVIII as a gift to the Spanish court.

The Five Senses Tea Service

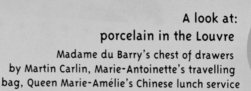

A look at:
porcelain in the Louvre
Madame du Barry's chest of drawers by Martin Carlin, Marie-Antoinette's travelling bag, Queen Marie-Amélie's Chinese lunch service

Heroes and heroism: battle painting

By March 30th, 1814, the enemy had reached the gates of Paris. Wooden palisades were hastily put up around the city, like those at the barrier at Clichy. It was here that soldiers of the Garde Nationale fought to the death in a last-ditch attempt to resist the advancing Russians. In the heat of battle, amidst the incessant gunfire and booming cannons, the thick, acrid dust has concealed the sky. Did Horace Vernet listen to military fanfares whilst painting this picture? He often did in his studio in the Jeu de Paume in Versailles, where he painted his huge battle scenes. Having joined the Garde Nationale with his father out of loyalty to the Emperor, Vernet fought at Clichy, and has included himself among the recognisable people next to Maréchal Moncey, the Garde's commander, giving orders on horseback. The picture extols the heroism and patriotism of the French, but its huge public success was due to its profusion of realistic, tragic and moving details with which Vernet, like a serial writer, studded the canvas with: the trembling peasant women clutching her baby, the bloody linen covering the wounds, etc. He had the knack of telling both the 'big' story and the 'little' stories it is comprised of, without this profusion of detail interfering with the overall composition, and breathed new life into classical military and history painting genre, which remained popular throughout the 19th century.

A look at:
19th-century France in the Louvre
Napoleon Ist on the battlefield at Eylau by Antoine-Jean Gros, *Liberty Leading the People* by Eugène Delacroix, the sculpture, *Lion Fighting a Serpent* by Antoine-Louis Barye

Defending the Barrier at Clichy